First published 2004 by Kingfisher

This edition published 2013 by Macmillan Children's Books
a division of Macmillan Publishers Limited
20 New Wharf Road, London N1 9RR
Basingstoke and Oxford
Associated companies throughout the world
www.panmacmillan.com

ISBN 978-1-4472-5007-4

1 3 5 7 9 8 6 4 2

A CIP catalogue record for this book is available from the British Library.

Printed and bound by CPI Group (UK) Ltd, Croydon CR0 4YY

SERIOUSLY SILLY SCHOOL JOKES

A BONKERS BOOK OF THE BEST SCHOOL JOKES

Illustrated by Tony Trimmer

MACMILLAN CHILDREN'S BOOKS

Teacher: Sunil, have you given the fish in the aquarium any fresh water?

Sunil: No, miss, they haven't drunk this lot yet.

Teacher: If you had £2 in one pocket and £4 in the other, what would you have altogether, Tom?

Tom: Someone else's jeans, sir.

Teacher: You're late. You should have been here at 9 o'clock.
Pupil: Why? Did something happen?

Teacher: Give me three collective nouns.
Pupil: Wastepaper basket, vacuum cleaner and a dustpan.

Teacher: Can anyone tell me where elephants can be found?
Pupil: Don't be silly, sir, they're much too big to lose.

Joanne: Dad, can you write in the dark?
Dad: Sure I can. What do you want me to write?
Joanne: Your name on my report card.

Why did the teacher send Dracula's son home?

Because he was coffin so much.

What did the ghost teacher say to her pupils?

"Now look at the board, while I go through it again."

Teacher: What's the difference between an Indian elephant and an African elephant?
Pupil: About 3000 miles.

How do teachers dress in winter?
Quickly.

What's the difference between a teacher and a steam train?
One says, "Spit out that chewing gum," and the other says, "Choo-choo!"

What stands in the middle of Paris?
The letter "r".

Gareth went to the school tuck shop and bought an ice lolly at lunchtime. He hadn't quite finished it before he went into his geography lesson so he stuffed it in his trouser pocket. The teacher asked the class, "What do we call people living in China?"

"Chinese, miss."

"What do we call people living in America?"

"American."

"Now, Gareth, since all you seem to be doing is fiddling with your pocket, can you tell me what we call people living in Europe?"

"Er, no . . . miss."

"European," shouted a voice from the back of the class.

"No, I'm not," said Gareth. "My ice lolly's melted."

Gareth: I'm sorry I'm late for school, sir, but I was having a dream about football.
Teacher: Why does having a dream about football make you late for school?
Gareth: They played extra time.

How can a teacher double her money?
By folding it in half.

Teacher: Why were the Pilgrim Fathers called the early settlers?
Pupil: Because they paid their bills promptly?

What are the two good things about being a teacher?
July and August.

Why was the head teacher worried?

Because there were so many rulers in the school.

Teacher: What did it say on the door of the Pharaoh's tomb?
Pupil: Toot 'n' come in.

Why did the teacher turn on the lights?
Because her pupils were so dim.

$$1 + 1 = 11$$

Yasmin: I wish I'd lived a long time ago.
Teacher: Why?
Yasmin: Then I'd have less history to learn.

Mr Hancock: Who can tell me what the Scots mean by "lads and lasses"?

Jasvir: I know, sir, lads are boys and lassies are dogs!

Teacher: If you had five chocolate bars and your little brother asked you for one, how many would you have left?
Pupil: Five, of course!

Why can't executioners learn French?
Because they know no merci.

Headteacher at assembly: Last night someone broke into the school stationery cupboard and stole a load of blunt pencils. The police described the theft as pointless.

Why did the boy take a ladder to school?
Because it was a high school.

Robert: Why are you sitting in the gerbil's cage?
Kashif: Because I want to be the teacher's pet!

Why do head teachers never look out of the window in the mornings?
Because they wouldn't have anything to do in the afternoons.

What do you call someone who keeps on talking when no one is listening?
A teacher!

Teacher: Why do birds fly south in winter?
Pupil: Because it's too far to walk.

Teacher: Gavin, don't hum while you're working.
Gavin: I'm not working, miss, just humming.

Teacher: Where are you from?
Pupil: America, miss.
Teacher: Which part?
Pupil: All of me, miss!

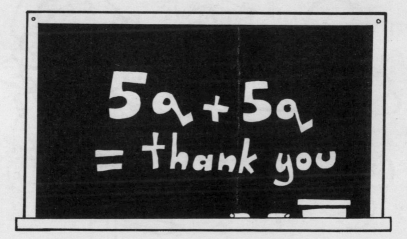

Teacher: What's 5q and 5q?
Paolo: 10q.
Teacher: You're welcome!

Why did the children eat sweets in class?

Because their teacher told them not to.

Teacher: If I had five apples in one hand, and six in another, what would I have?

Pupil: Big hands, sir.

What's the best thing about going to school?
Coming home again.

Teacher: You've got your shoes on the wrong feet.
Small boy: These are the only feet I've got, miss.

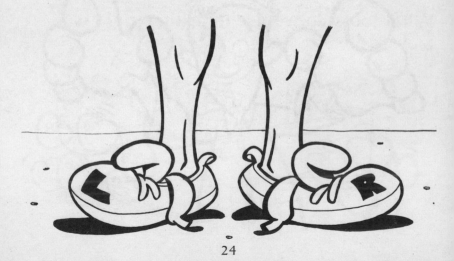

At a school nativity play the three wise men came onto the stage. The first wise man put an envelope down in front of the crib. "Leo!" said the teacher. "You are supposed to give the baby Jesus gold!"

"Yes, miss," said Leo, "but this is a Manchester United season ticket – my dad says they are just like gold!"

What tools do we use in arithmetic?
Multipliers!

Teacher: Sarah, what's twelve times twelve?

Sarah: A hundred and forty-four.

Teacher: Good.

Sarah: Good, miss? It's perfect!

Teacher: If I bought one hundred buns for 10p, what would each bun be?

Pupil: Stale.

What kind of tree does a maths teacher climb?
A geometry.

Teacher: You have a fine voice, Darren, but please don't spoil it by singing!

There was once a very intelligent boy. Whenever he got a good school report his father would give him 20p and a pat on the head. By the time he was twelve he had £50 and a very flat head.

Teacher: What's your favourite song?
Pupil: *I have five: "Three Blind Mice" and "Tea for Two".*

Robert: Sarah, you're stupid!
Sarah: Boo-hoo . . . sob . . . sniff.
**Teacher: Robert, that was very
unkind, say you're sorry at once.**
Robert: Sorry you're stupid, Sarah.

**Maths teacher: Oscar, how
many times have I told you
to stop playing with that
calculator?**
Oscar: Er . . . 6,340 times, sir!

"My teacher brought a maths plant to school this morning."
"What do you mean?"
"She said it had square roots."

Why did the boy take his car to school?
To drive his teacher up the wall.

Teacher: Why are you standing on your head?
Pupil: I'm just turning things over in my mind, miss.

Teacher: What do you call the outside of a tree?
Boy: I don't know, miss.
Teacher: Bark.
Boy: Woof!

Chemistry teacher: What are nitrates?
Pupil: I don't know, but I expect they are cheaper than day rates.

Why did the teacher wear sunglasses?
Because her pupils were so bright.

$$E = Mc^2$$

PE teacher: There are only two things stopping you from becoming the greatest athlete in the world, David.
David: What are they, sir?
PE teacher: Your feet, dear!

Teacher: What's the most important thing to remember in a chemistry lesson?
Pupil: Don't lick the spoon.

What do you call two people who embarrass you at Parents' Evening?
Mum and Dad!

Mother: Why are you home from school so early, Tom?

Tom: Because I was the only one who could answer a tricky question.

Mother: Oh, really? What was the question?

Tom: Who threw the pencil at the headmaster?

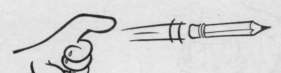

Teacher: How would you spell "amphibian"?

Pupil: I wouldn't, miss, I would spell "frog".

Little Sally in Year 1 told her mum that she had broken off her engagement to her friend Carlo.

"Oh dear, why?" said her mum.

"Well," cried Sally, "I don't think he was ready for me *and* he scribbled in my colouring book!"

"Mummy, the other children at school keep calling me a bighead."

"Don't worry, darling, there's nothing in it."

Dad: How are your marks at school?

Son: They're underwater.

Dad: What?

Son: They're below C!

"Is your school dinner spicy?"

*"No, smoke always comes out of my
ears."*

"I won a prize at school today, Mummy,"
said Emily. "Miss Trubsham asked how
many legs an elephant has got, and I
said, 'Three.'"
"Three?" said Mum. "Then how did
you win the prize?"
"I was closest," said Emily.

Why did the cell cross the microscope?
To get to the other slide.

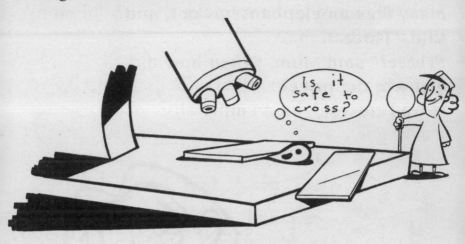

Teacher: Who invented fractions?
Student: Henry the Eighth.

Teacher: For all those who were late this morning because they stayed up to watch the football, we're going to make the school more like a football match.

Pupils: Hooray!

Teacher: So you can all stay behind and do extra time tonight, as a penalty.

Pupils: Boo!

What's the worst thing you're likely to find in the school canteen?

The food.

Teacher: Why did knights in armour practise a lot?
Pupil: To stop them getting rusty, sir.

What do you call the small rivers that run into the Nile?
Juveniles.

Teacher: Can anyone tell me the name of the Dog Star?
Pupil: Lassie.

What kind of food do maths teachers eat?
Square meals.

*"Please miss, there was a
frog in Donna's burger."*
**"Well, can't Donna
speak for herself?"**
*"No, miss, she's got the
frog in her throat now!"*

**Why were the naughty
eggs sent out of class?**
*Because they kept playing
practical yolks.*

Teacher: Sam, why were you late for school this morning?

Sam: Well, the alarm was set for seven, but there are eight in our family.

What's the difference between school dinners and dog food?

School dinners come on plates.

Teacher: Sadie, why are you crawling to school ten minutes late?
Sadie: Because you told me never to walk in late again.

Teacher: I hope I didn't see you looking at Fred's exam paper.
Pupil: I hope you didn't either!

How many rotten eggs
did the school cook put
into the omelettes?
A phew.

Teacher: Why were you late for
school, Ronan?
Ronan: I was stopping two boys fighting, sir.
Teacher: Excellent. How did you stop them?
Ronan: I kicked them both, sir!

Get in the Saddle — E. C. Rider

Parachuting — Hugo First

Abracadabra — Wiz Ard

They Came from Uranus — I. M. Rude

Sweeping Beauty — I. M. A. Cleaner

Stop the Bus — Isa Coming

Making Friends — I. Malone

Dying for the Loo — Phil Mépants

Outside the Headmaster's Office — Watts E. Dunn

School Dinners — Buster Gutt

Rapping made Easy — M. E. Nem

When Shall We Meet Again?
Miles Apart

The Arctic Ocean
I.C. Waters

The Policeman's Rule Book
Laura Norda

A Load of Rubbish
Stefan Nonsense

She Came from Outer Space
Aileen B. Ing

At the Bottom of the Cliff
Eileen Dover

Playing for Real
D. Beckham

What's Growing in the Garden?
Rose Bush

Pupil: I thought we had a choice for dinner but there's only salad.
Dinner lady: That's the choice, take it or leave it!

Angry teacher: Didn't you hear me call you?
Pupil: But you told me not to answer back.

Teacher: Why are you always late for school, Jane?
Jane: Because you keep ringing the bell before I get here, miss.

Dinner lady: Eat up your greens, they're good for your skin.
Pupil: But I don't want green skin!

Dad: Do you want some help with your homework, Danny?

Danny: No thanks, Dad, I'll get it wrong on my own.

Pupil 1, outside dining hall: Oh good, we're having salad today.

Pupil 2: How do you know it's salad?

Pupil 1: Well, I can't smell anything burning.

Art teacher: I asked you to draw a picture of a cow eating grass. Why have you handed in a blank piece of paper?

Pupil: Because the cow ate all the grass, so there's no grass to draw any more.

Art teacher: But where is the cow?

Pupil: What's the point in the cow hanging around if there's no grass to eat?

Teacher: Your homework story "My Dog" is exactly the same, word for word, as your brother's.
Pupil: I know, miss, it's the same dog.

Teacher: Maria, you've been doing Sam's homework again. I recognise your writing in his book.

Maria: No, I haven't, miss. It's just we both used the same pencil.

Teacher: How do you like doing your homework?

Pupil: I like doing nothing better!

Lizzie: Dad, I'm tired of doing my homework.
Dad: Come on now, homework never killed anyone.
Lizzie: I know, but I don't want to be the first.

Pupil: Would you punish me for something I didn't do?
Teacher: Of course not.
Pupil: Good, because I haven't done my homework.

Anne: Sir, why have
you got a sausage
behind your ear?
*Mr James: Oh no,
I must have eaten
my pencil for lunch!*

What's the difference between school dinners and horse poo?
School dinners are usually cold.

A vampire's school report:
English: Good.
Maths: Good.
Cricket: Shows promise as a bat.

Teacher: Give me a sentence with "I" in it.
Pupil: I is . . .
Teacher: No, you should always say "I am . . ."
Pupil: I am the ninth letter of the alphabet!

"Your report is disgraceful, Fred," said his father. "And what's more, it says you're very careless about your appearance."
"Really, Dad?"
"Yes, it says you haven't appeared at school for three weeks."

Teacher: Write the longest sentence you can.
Pupil: Easy! "Life imprisonment".

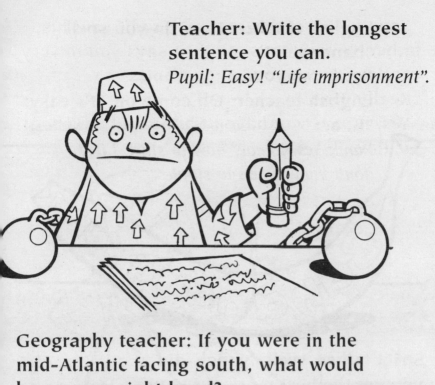

Geography teacher: If you were in the mid-Atlantic facing south, what would be on your right hand?
Pupil: Four fingers and a thumb, miss.

English teacher: How do you spell "banana"?

Pupil: I'm not sure.

English teacher: Oh come on, it's easy: "B, a..."

Pupil: Yes, I know how to start, I just don't know when to stop!

Strict father: Well, Nancy, did you get the best marks in your class this term?

Nancy: No, Dad. Did you get the best salary in your office?

Benito came home from school with his end-of-term report.

"Guess what, Dad. I've got some great news for you."

His dad looked pleased. Benito said, "You remember you promised me £10 if I had a good report?"

"Yes," said his father, reaching for his wallet.

"You'll be pleased to hear that you don't have to pay me!"

Teacher: Give me a sentence with the word "centimetre" in it.

Pupil: My gran came to stay and I was sent t'meet 'er!

Teacher: Name me two days of the week that begin with "T".

Pupil: Today and tomorrow.

Tunday

Tonday

Triday

Tednesday

Year 6 was going to France on a cross-channel ferry. The head teacher was reminding them about safety on board.
"Now then, Year 6, what do you shout if a boy falls overboard?"
"Shout, 'Boy overboard!'" replied Michael.
"Correct," said the head teacher. "And what if a teacher falls overboard?"
"Shout, 'Hooray!'" replied Michael.

Teacher: Can anyone give me the name of a liquid that won't freeze?
Pupil: Hot water, sir.